THE GIANT BOOK OF CHRISTIAN

SHE
MU

PIANO · VOCAL · GUITAR

Alfred

Produced by
Alfred Music Publishing Co., Inc.
P.O. Box 10003
Van Nuys, CA 91410-0003
alfred.com

Printed in USA.

ISBN-10: 0-7390-9899-3

ISBN-13: 978-0-7390-9899-8

Cover image: Celtic cross © Shutterstock.com / vectorbomb

Contents

10,000 Reasons

(Bless the Lord)

Words and Music by
MATT REDMAN and JONAS MYRIN

Verse 1 (Sing 1st time only):

Verse 2 (Sing 2nd time only):

Chorus:

AMAZING GRACE
(My Chains Are Gone)

Words and Music by
CHRIS TOMLIN and LOUIE GIGLIO

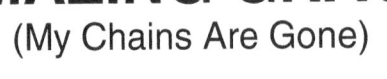

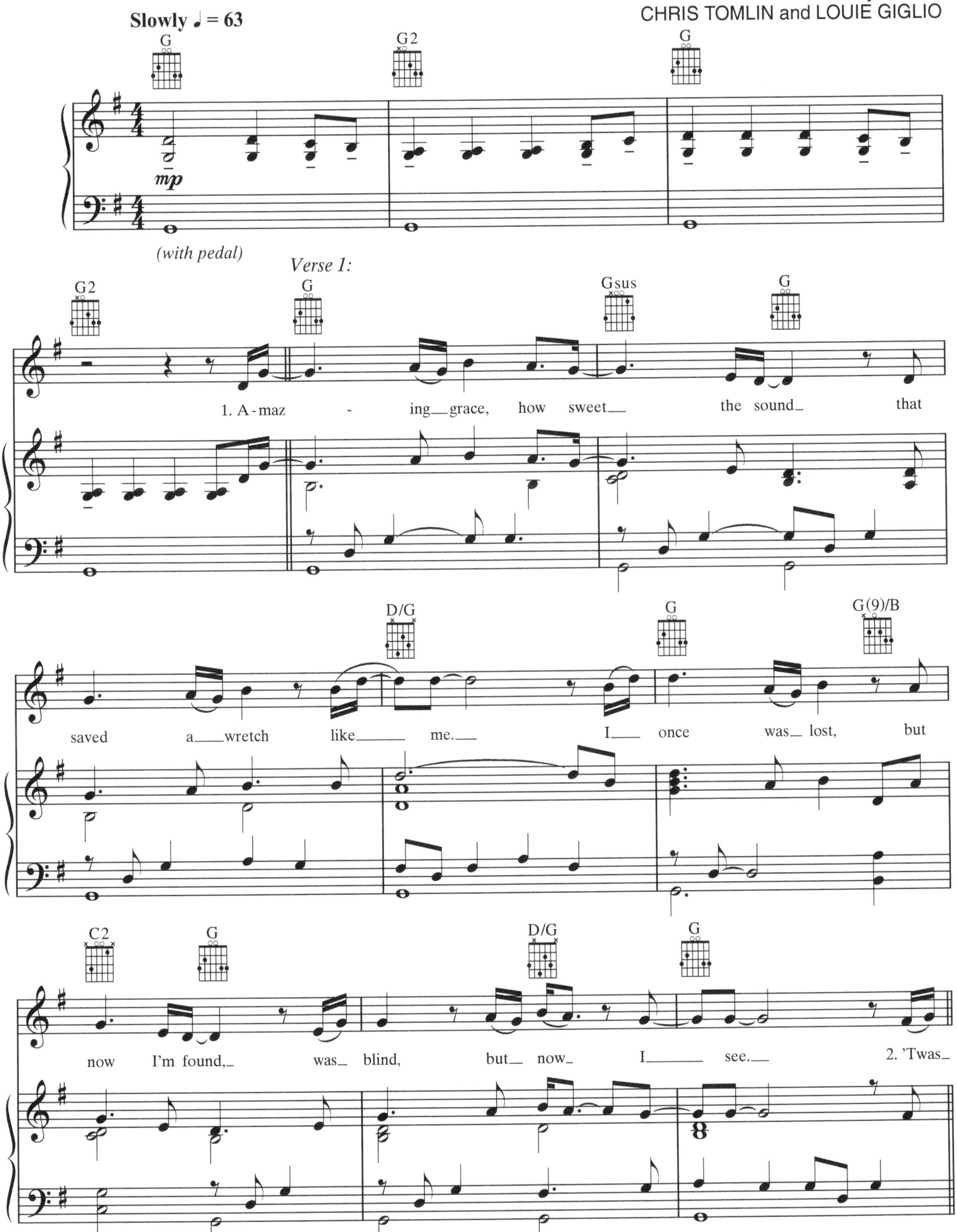

Slowly ♩ = 63
G
G2
G
mp
(with pedal)
Verse 1:
G2
G
Gsus
G
1. A-maz - ing grace, how sweet the sound that
D/G
G
G(9)/B
saved a wretch like me. I once was lost, but
C2
G
D/G
G
now I'm found, was blind, but now I see.
2. 'Twas

Verse 2:

Verse 4:

ABOVE ALL

Words and Music by
PAUL BALOCHE
and LENNY LEBLANC

Chorus:

Cru - ci - fied,___ laid be - hind___ the stone,___ You

lived to die,___ re - ject - ed and___ a - lone.___ Like a rose___

___ tram-pled on___ the ground,_____ You took__ the fall___ and thought of me__

D.S. %

a - bove__ all.

A-bove all_____

AMAZING GRACE

TRADITIONAL

Amazing Grace - 2 - 1

BLESSINGS

Words and Music by
LAURA MIXON STORY

sand sleep - less nights_ are what_ it takes__ to know_ You're near?_

And what if trials_ of__ this life___ are Your mer - cies in___ dis - guise?_

Verse 2:

2. We pray_ for wis - dom,___ Your voice_ to hear._

Bridge:

When friends be - tray___ us, when dark - ness seems___ to win,___ we___ know that pain___ re - minds___ this heart___ that this is not,___ this is not___ our home.___ It's not___ our___ home.___

Chorus:

BLESSED

Words and Music by
BILLIE HUGHES

Verse 1:

1. If ev - er___ you lose___ your way,

to find you have no place to stand.

And you spread your tan - gled

34

those who   wait up - on   the Lord.

CINDERELLA

Words and Music by
STEVEN CURTIS CHAPMAN

44

— in my arms,___ 'cause I know

some-thing the prince___ nev - er knew._____ Oh,_____

_____ I will dance___ with Cin - der - el - la. I don't

want to miss___ e - ven one___ song, 'cause all too___

soon the clock will strike___ mid - night___

and she'll be

gone.___

GOD'S NOT DEAD (Like a Lion)

Words and Music by
DANIEL BASHTA

C
E
I'll o - ver - come. My God's
N.C.
Chorus:
Em
G♯m
not dead, He's sure - ly a - live. He's liv - ing on the in - side,
D
F♯
roar-ing like a li - on. God's not dead, He's sure - ly a - live. He's liv -
Em
G♯m
Cmaj7
Emaj7
Em7
G♯m7
ing on the in - side, roar-ing like a li - on. Roar - ing, He's roar-

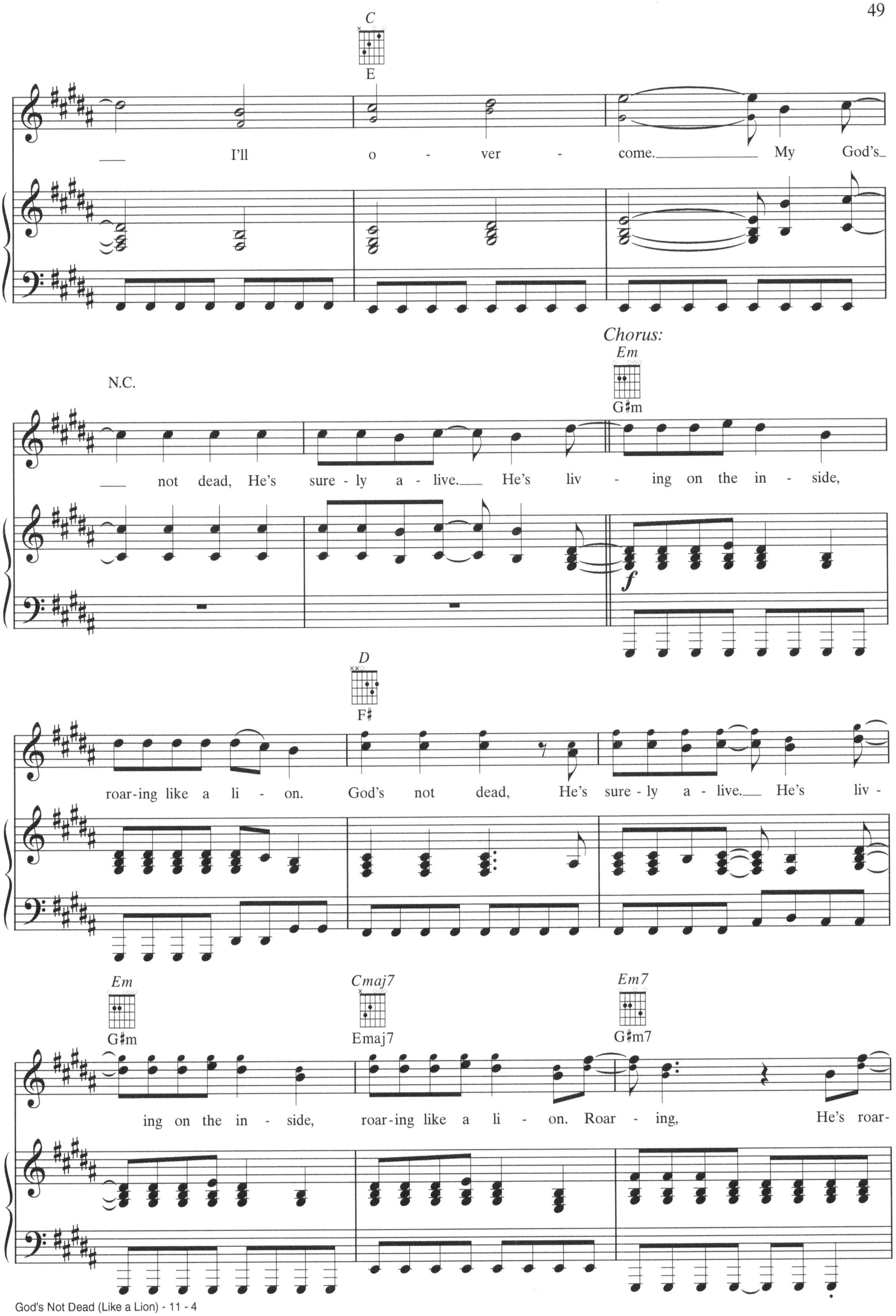

Em7
G♯m7
Come shake the ground with the sound of re -
Am
C♯m
G
B
viv - al. Let Heav - en roar
D/F♯
F♯/A♯
and fi - re fall.
Come shake the
Em7
G♯m7
Am
C♯m
ground with the sound of re - viv - al.

54

Lyrics beneath the staves:

ing like a li - on. God's not dead, He's sure-ly a-live.__ He's liv-

ing on the in - side, roar-ing like a li - on. God's not dead, He's sure-

ly a-live.__ He's liv - ing on the in - side, roar-ing like a li - on.

God's not dead, He's sure-ly a-live.__ He's liv - ing on the in - side,

I WILL RISE

Words and Music by
CHRIS TOMLIN, JESSE REEVES,
LOUIE GIGLIO and MATT MAHER

Moderately slow ♩ = 84

(with pedal)

Verse 1:

1. There's a peace I've come__ to know,__ though my heart and flesh__ may fail.__ There's an an-chor for__ my soul.__ I can say,__

62

I Will Rise - 7 - 6

GOOD MORNING

Words and Music by
AARON RICE, CARY BARLOWE, JAMIE MOORE,
MANDISA HUNDLEY and TOBY MCKEEHAN

Good Morning - 8 - 1

HOLD ME

Words and Music by
CHRIS STEVENS, JAMIE GRACE
and TOBY McKEEHAN

Moderately bright reggae feel ♩ = 136

I love, I love, I love, I love the way You hold_ me.

I love, I love, I love, I love the way You hold_ me. I love, I love, I love, I

love the way You hold_ me. I love, I love, I love, I love the way You, the way You...

* Guitar capo at 4th fret.

world is gon - na bring me down, that's when Your smile__ comes a - round. Ooh, I love the way You

fig - ure You out,__ You make me wan - na sing and shout. I love the way You

Chorus:

hold me. By__ my side You'll al - ways be. You take each and ev - 'ry day, make it spe - cial in__

__ some way. I love the way You hold me. In__ Your arms I'll al - ways be. You take each and ev -

Chorus:

B7   F#   G#m7

hold me. By__ my side You'll al-ways be. You take each and ev - 'ry day, make it spec-ial in__

E   B7   F#

__ some way. I love the way You hold me. In__ Your arms I'll al-ways be. You take each and ev -

G#m7   E   B7

'ry day, ev-'ry day, ev - 'ry day. I love the way You hold me. By__ my side You'll

F#   G#m7   E

al-ways be. You take each and ev - 'ry day, oh,__ so spe - cial. I love the way You

Hold Me - 8 - 6

79

Hold Me - 8 - 8

HOW BEAUTIFUL

Words and Music by
TWILA PARIS

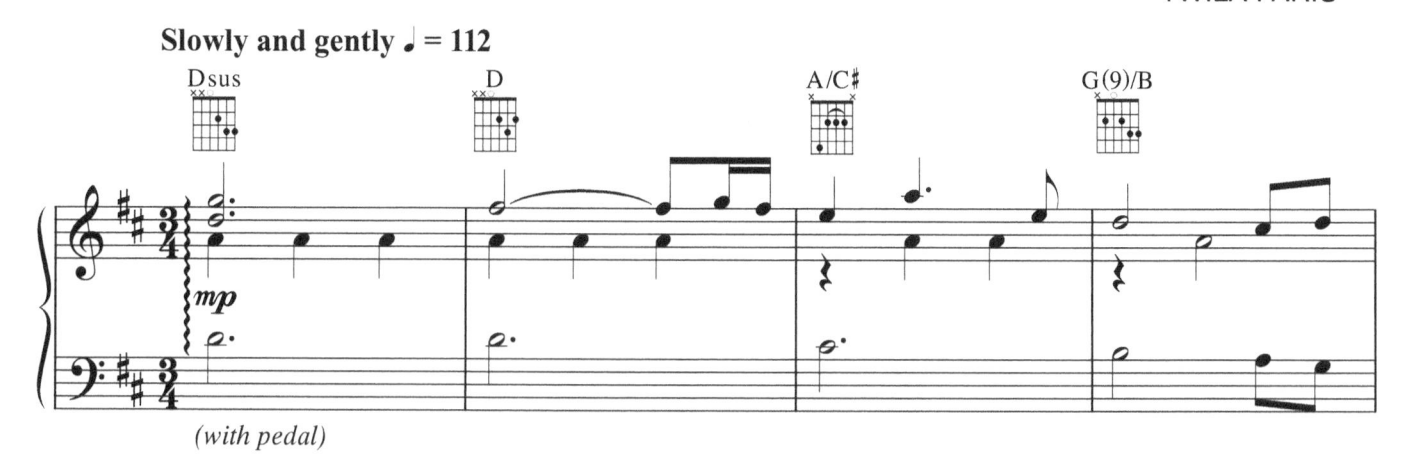

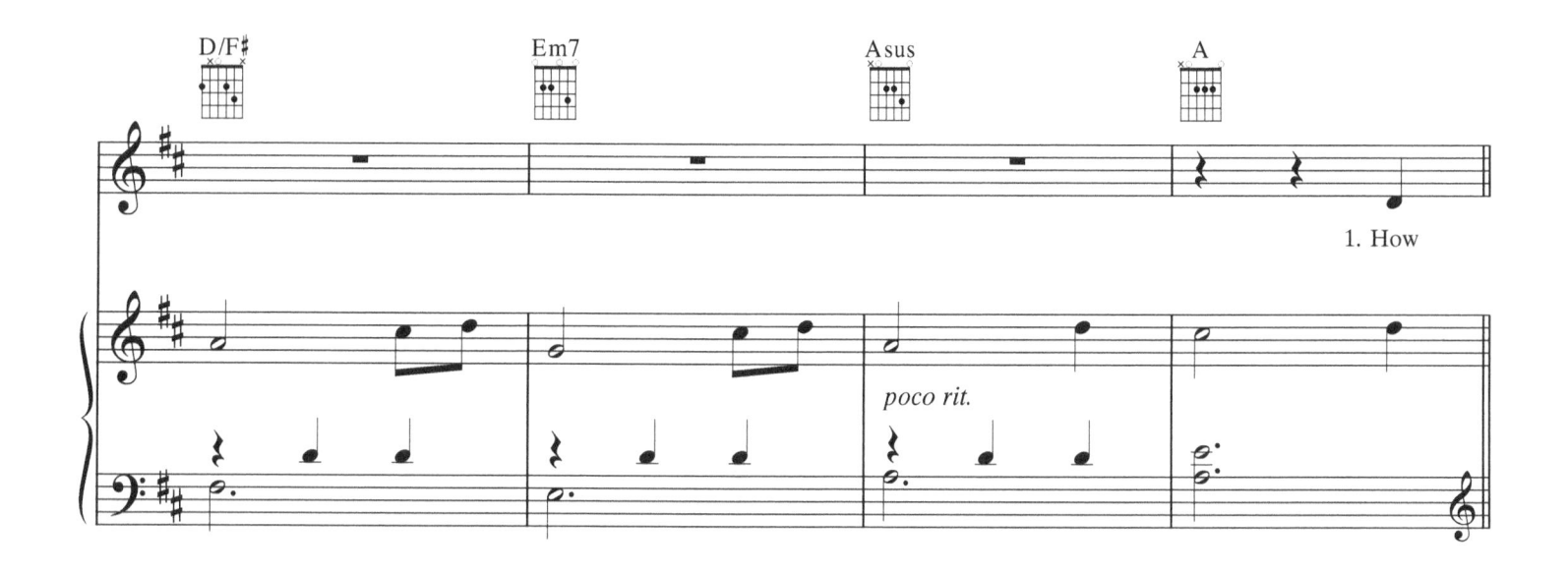

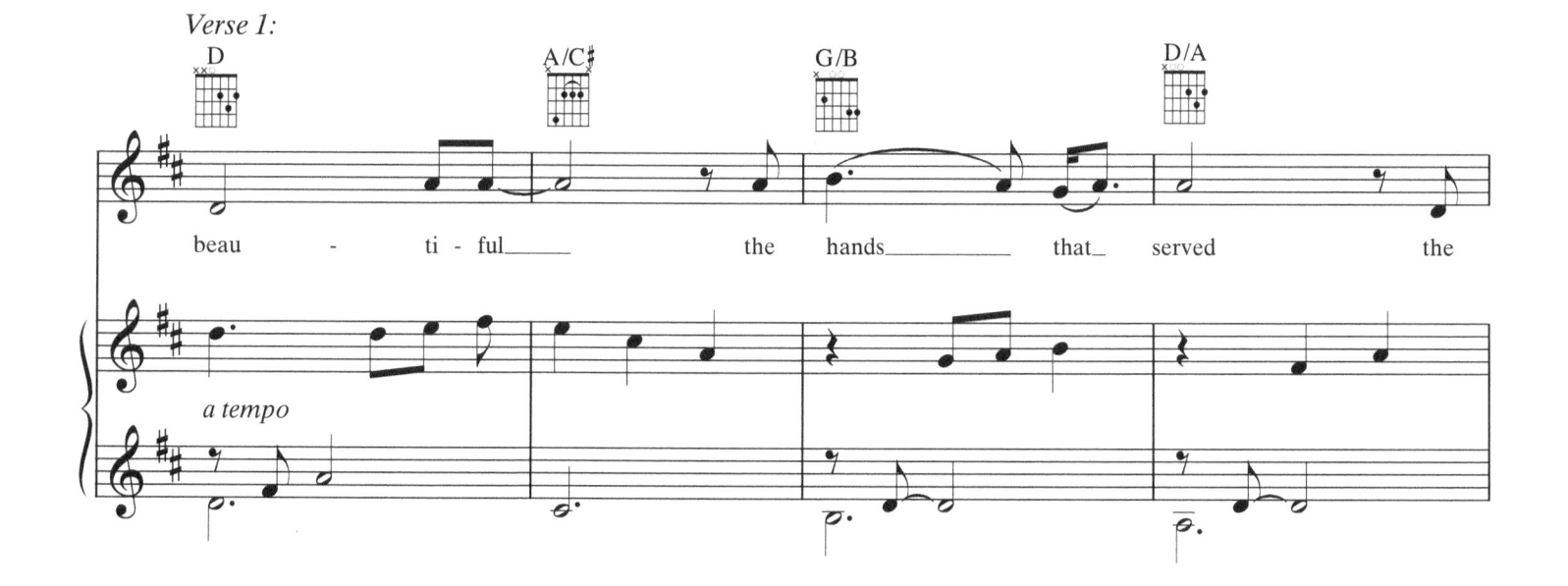

died,   will-ing to   pay   the price,

will-ing to   pay   the price.

Verse 3:

3. How beau - ti - ful   the

rit. e dim.   *p*   *mp*
a tempo

88

feet that___ bring___ the sound of good___ news and the

love of___ the King. How___ beau - ti - ful the

hands___ that_ serve the wine and the bread___ and the

Chorus:

sons_ of the_ earth. How___ beau - ti - ful,___

poco rit. *a tempo*

Amaj7　　　B　　　A/C#　　　B/D#

how___ beau - ti - ful,_____

Esus　　　E　　　B/D#　　A/C#　　B/D#

how___ beau - ti - ful_____

A/C#　　　B　　　Esus　　　E　　　B/D#

___ is the bod-y___ of Christ._____

rit. e dim.　　　*mp*　　　*a tempo*

A/C#　　　E/G#　　　F#m7　　　Bsus　　　B　　　E

rit. e dim.　　　*p*

HOW GREAT IS OUR GOD

Words and Music by
JESSE REEVES, CHRIS TOMLIN
and ED CASH

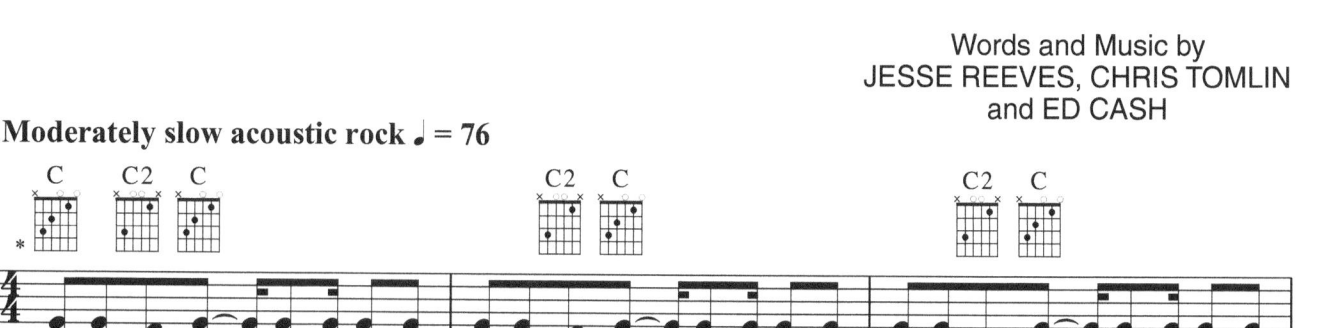

Verse 1 (sing 1st time only):

Verse 2 (sing 2nd time only):

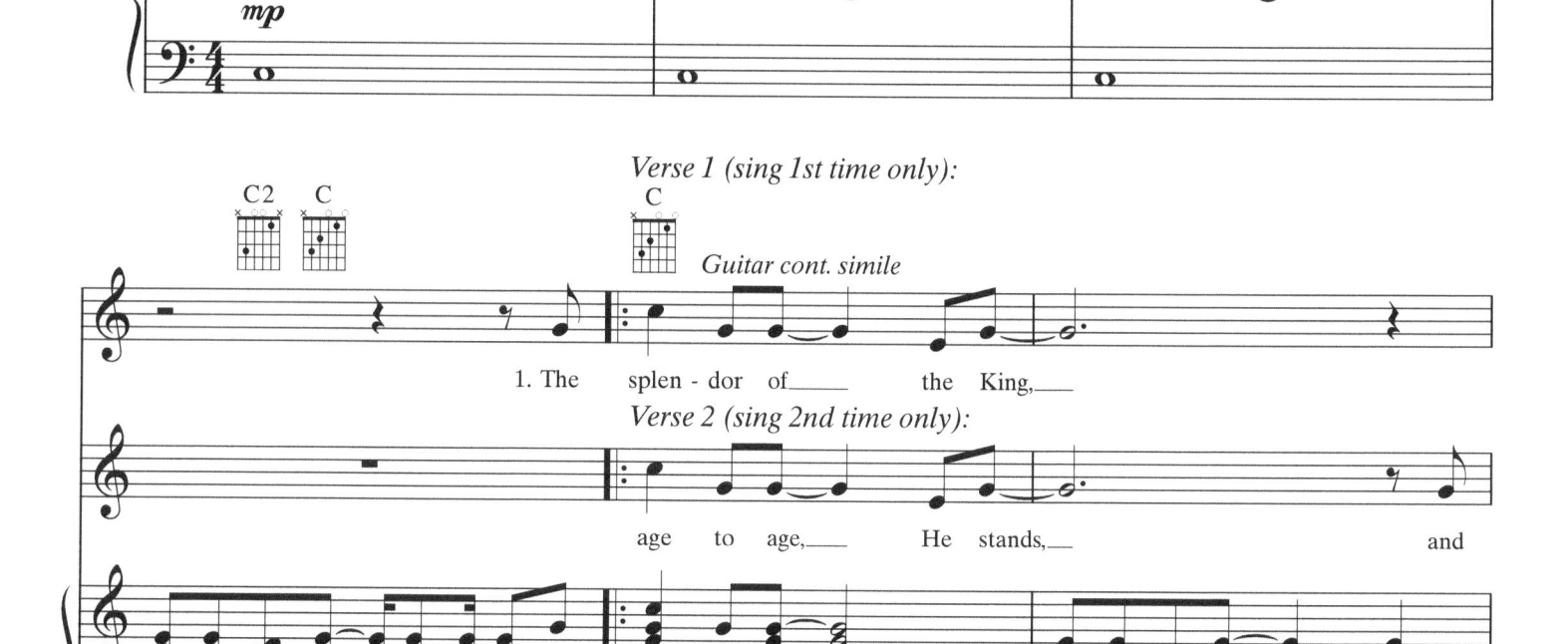

(play l.h. 2nd time)

*Original recording in D♭ major with Guitar Capo 1.

How Great Is Our God - 4 - 1

HOW HE LOVES

Words and Music by
JOHN MARK MCMILLAN

Verse 1:

Am7
C/G
Oh, oh, how He loves_ us,
C/F
how He_ loves us_ all.
C
Am7
C/F
Verse 2:
C
Am7
2. He is_ jea-lous for me,_ loves like a hur - ri-cane,
mf

98

for me. Oh,_____ how He loves!_____ Yeah, He

Chorus:

C   Am7

loves   us.   Oh,_____ how   He   loves   us.

C/G

Oh,_____ how   He   loves   us.   Oh,_____ how   He

Fmaj7   *Verse 3:*
                                                              C

loves._____   3. And   we are His   por - tion and

He is our prize,___ drawn to re-demp-tion by the grace in His eyes.___ If His

grace is an o-cean, we're all sink-ing.___

And heav-en meets earth like an un-fore-seen kiss and my

heart turns vio-lent-ly in-side of my chest. I don't have time to main -

I CAN ONLY IMAGINE

Words and Music by
BART MILLARD

ag - ine what my eyes___ will see when Your face___

is be - fore___ me. I can on - ly im - ag - ine.

Sur -

Chorus:

round - ed by___ Your glo - ry, what will my___ heart feel?___ Will I dance___

*Play l.h. Bass cues 2nd time (on D.S.).

I Can Only Imagine - 8 - 2

I NEED A MIRACLE

Words and Music by
DAVID CARR, MAC POWELL,
MARK LEE and TAI ANDERSON

Moderate rock ♩ = 83

Guitar Capo 2 →

Piano →

Verse 1:

1. Well, late___ one night,___ she start-ed to cry and thought,___

___ "He ain't com-in' home."___ She was tired___ of the lies, tired___ of the fight, but she

JESUS, FRIEND OF SINNERS

Words and Music by
MATTHEW WEST and MARK HALL

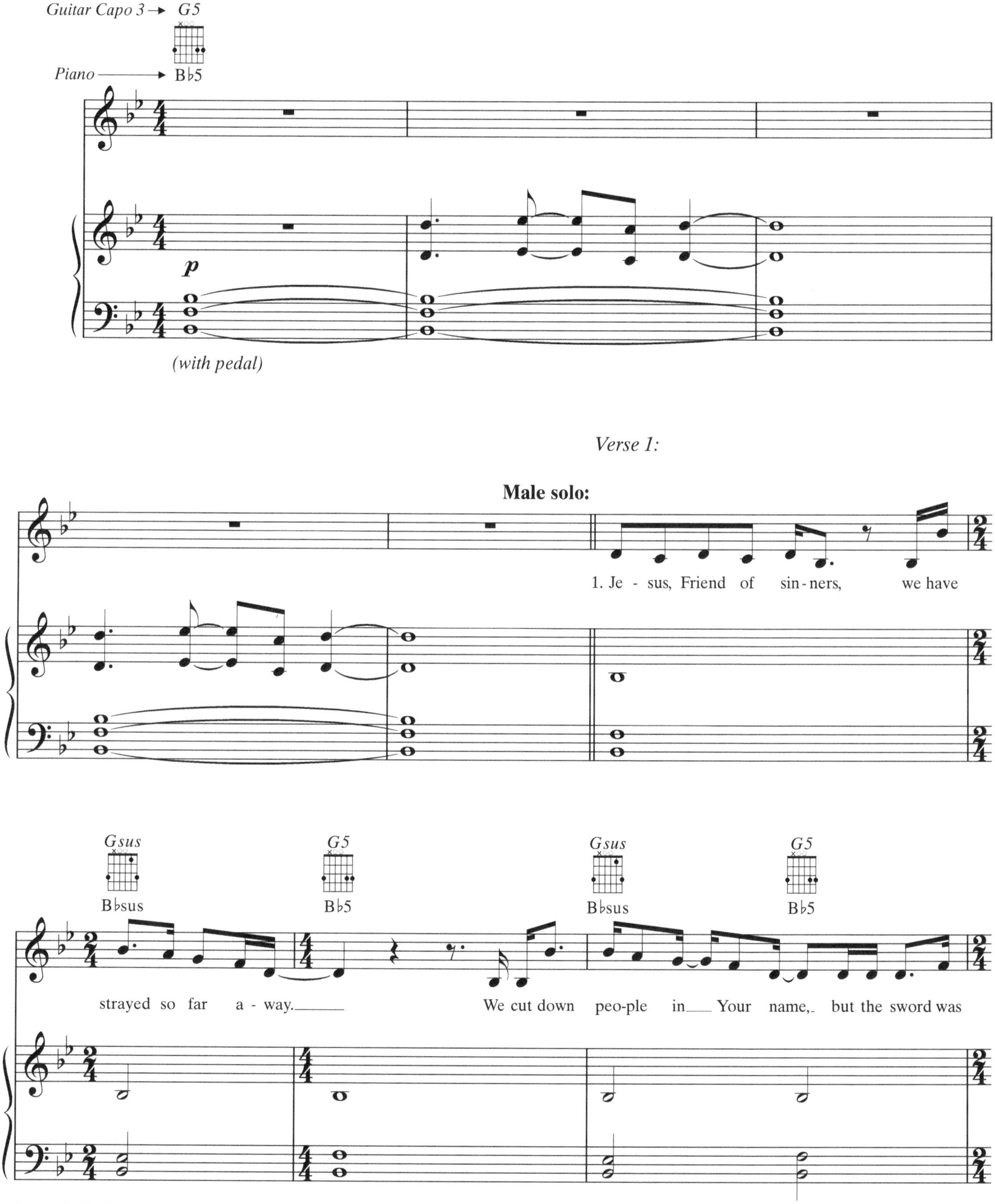

Verse 1:

Male solo:

1. Je - sus, Friend of sin - ners, we have

strayed so far a - way.___ We cut down peo-ple in___ Your name, but the sword was

Jesus, Friend of Sinners - 10 - 1

Chorus:

for, on-ly what we're a-gainst_ when we judge the wound-ed._____ What if we put down our

signs, crossed o-ver the lines_ and loved_ like You_ did?   Oh,_____

Chorus:

*Je - sus,   Friend of sin-ners,   o-pen our eyes_*

____ to the world at the end of our point-ing fin - gers.   Let our hearts_ be   led by

mer - cy. Help us reach with o - pen hearts _ and o - pen doors. _____ Oh,

Je - sus, Friend of sin - ners, break our hearts for what breaks _ Yours. _ You love ev-'ry

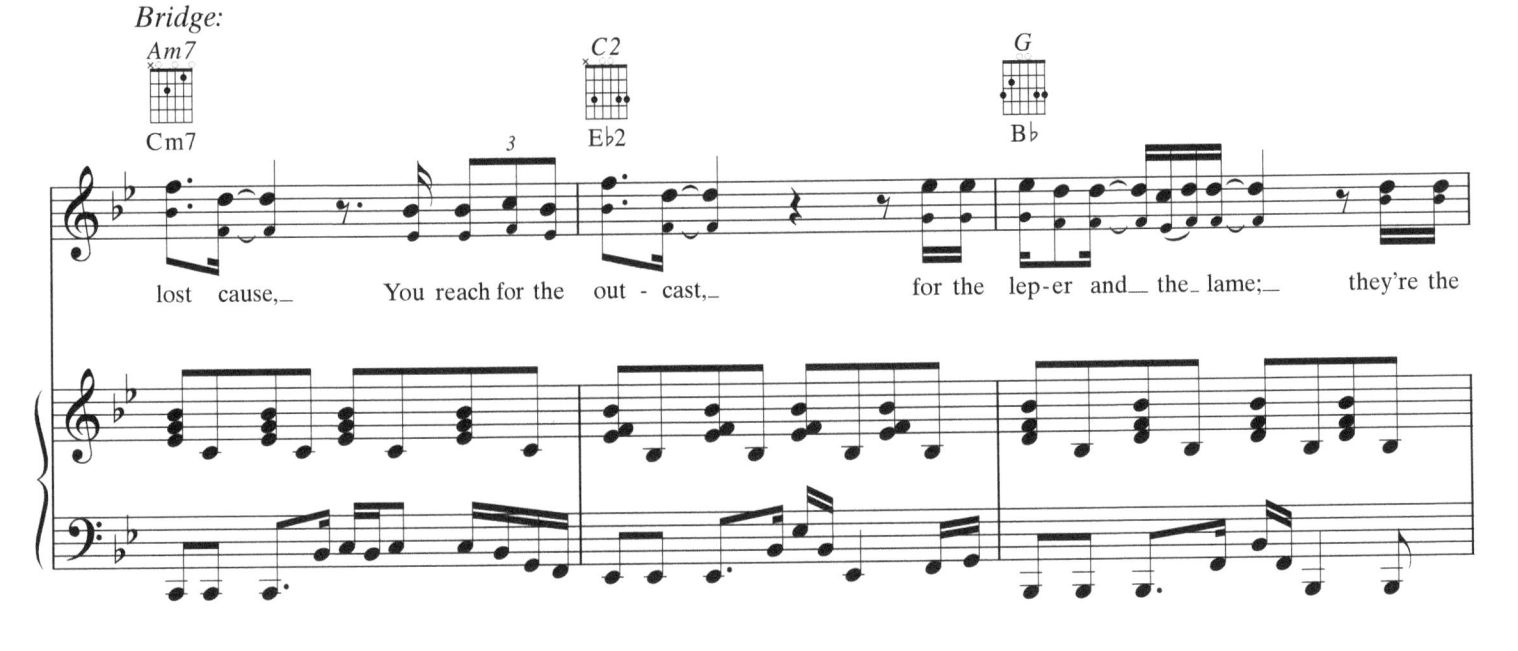

Bridge:

lost cause, _ You reach for the out - cast, _ for the lep-er and _ the _ lame; _ they're the

rea-son that_You came. Lord, I was that lost cause, and I was that out - cast,_ but You died for
(rea-son that_You came._____ I was that lost cause,_____ and I was the out - cast._)

sin-ners just_ like_ me,_ a grate-ful lep - er at_ Your feet._____ 'Cause You are_

good, You are_ good,____ and Your love en - dures for-

LET THE CHURCH SAY AMEN

Words and Music by
ANDRAÉ CROUCH

Let the Church Say Amen - 10 - 10

NEED YOU NOW (HOW MANY TIMES)

Words and Music by
CHRISTA WELLS, LUKE SHEETS
and TIFFANY ARBUCKLE

Slow pop groove ♩ = 66

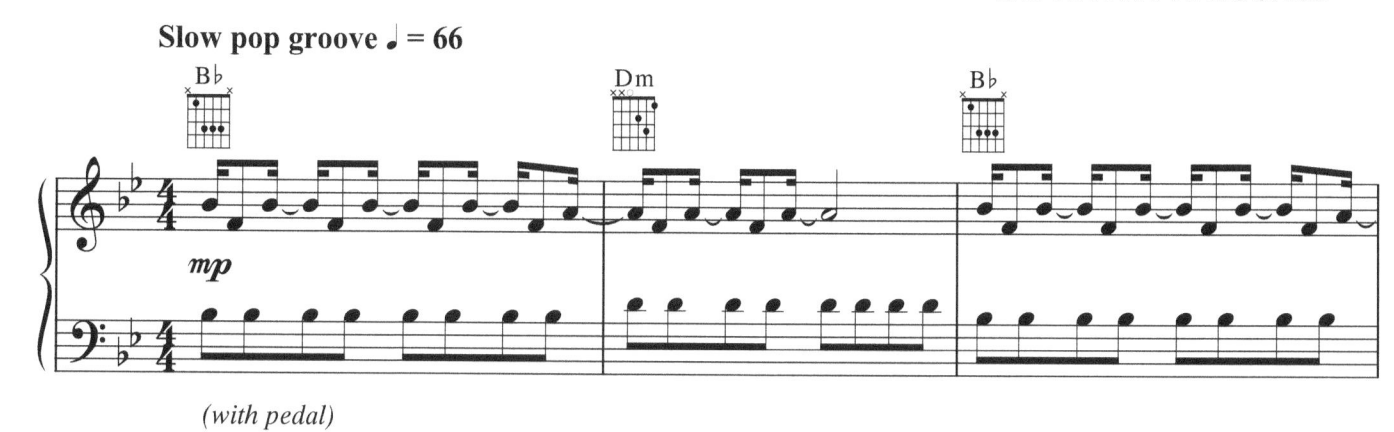

(with pedal)

Verse 1:

Need You Now - 6 - 1

140

ONE THING REMAINS

(Your Love Never Fails)

Words and Music by
JEREMY RIDDLE, BRIAN JOHNSON
and CHRISTA BLACK

THE PRAYER

Italian Lyric by
ALBERTO TESTA and TONY RENIS

Words and Music by
CAROLE BAYER SAGER and DAVID FOSTER

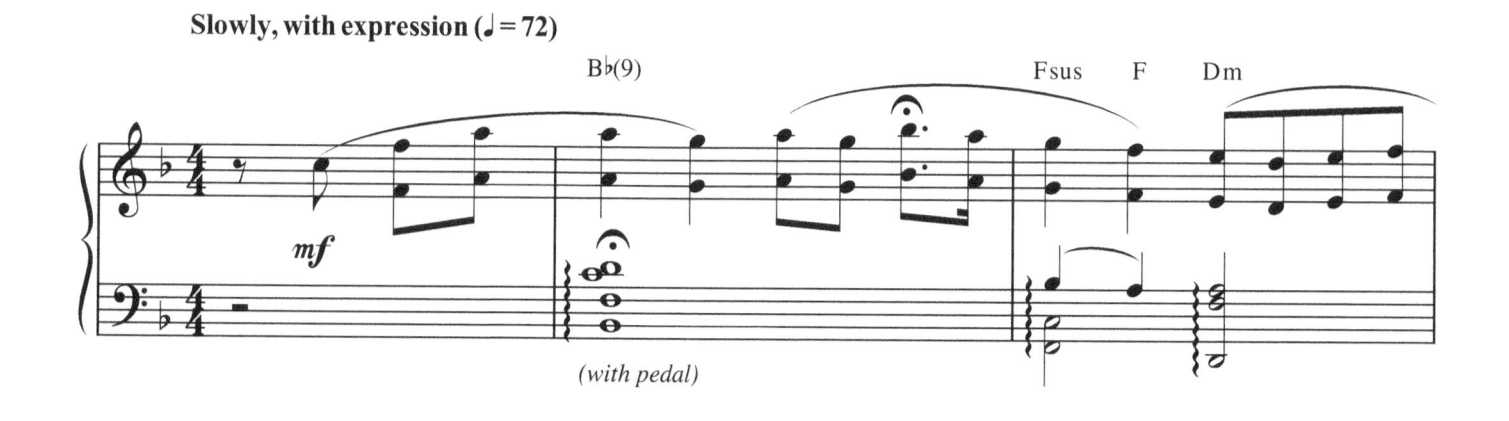

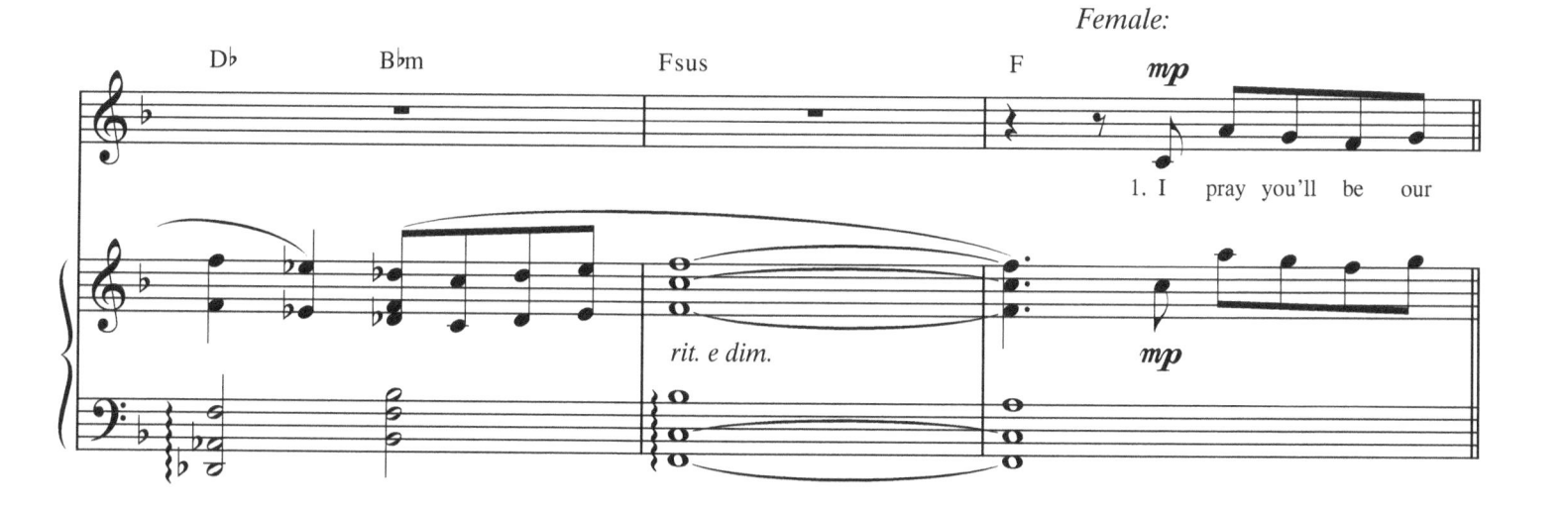

Verse 1:

Verse 3:

THE PROOF OF YOUR LOVE

Words and Music by
LUKE SMALLBONE, JOEL DAVID SMALLBONE,
BEN GLOVER, FREDERICK WILLIAMS,
JONATHAN LEE, and MIA FIELDES

The Proof of Your Love - 6 - 1

Chorus:

IN CHRIST ALONE

Words and Music by
STUART TOWNEND
and KEITH GETTY

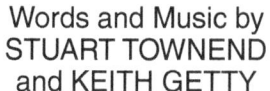

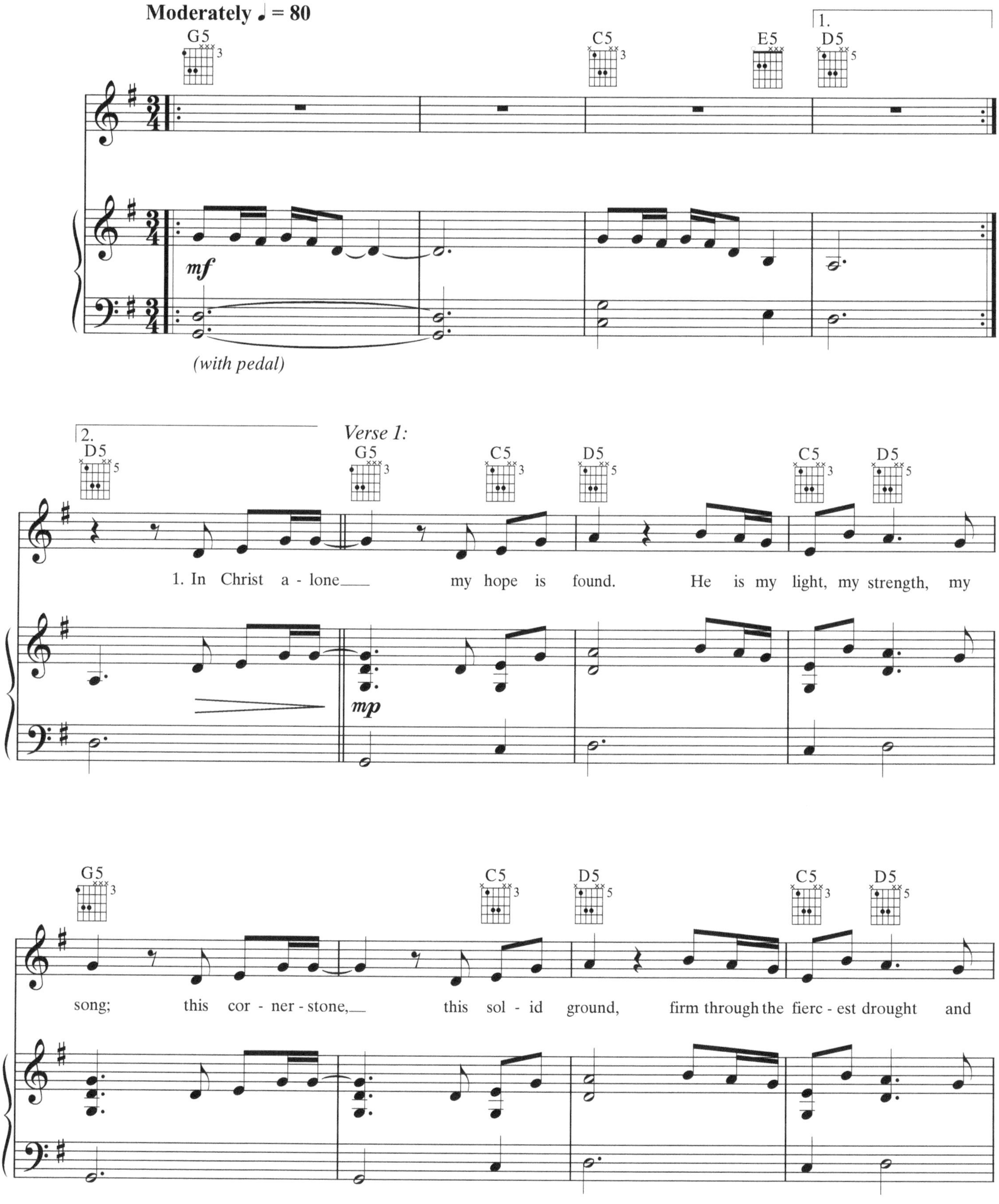
Moderately ♩ = 80
G5
C5
E5
1.
D5
mf
(with pedal)
2.
D5
Verse 1:
G5
C5
D5
C5
D5
1. In Christ a - lone my hope is found. He is my light, my strength, my
mp
G5
C5
D5
C5
D5
song; this cor - ner - stone, this sol - id ground, firm through the fierc - est drought and

Verse 3:

His bod-y lay, light of the world by dark-ness slain. Then, burst-ing

forth in glo-ri-ous day, up from the grave He rose a-gain. And as He

3.There in the ground

REDEEMED

Words and Music by
BENJI COWART and MICHAEL WEAVER

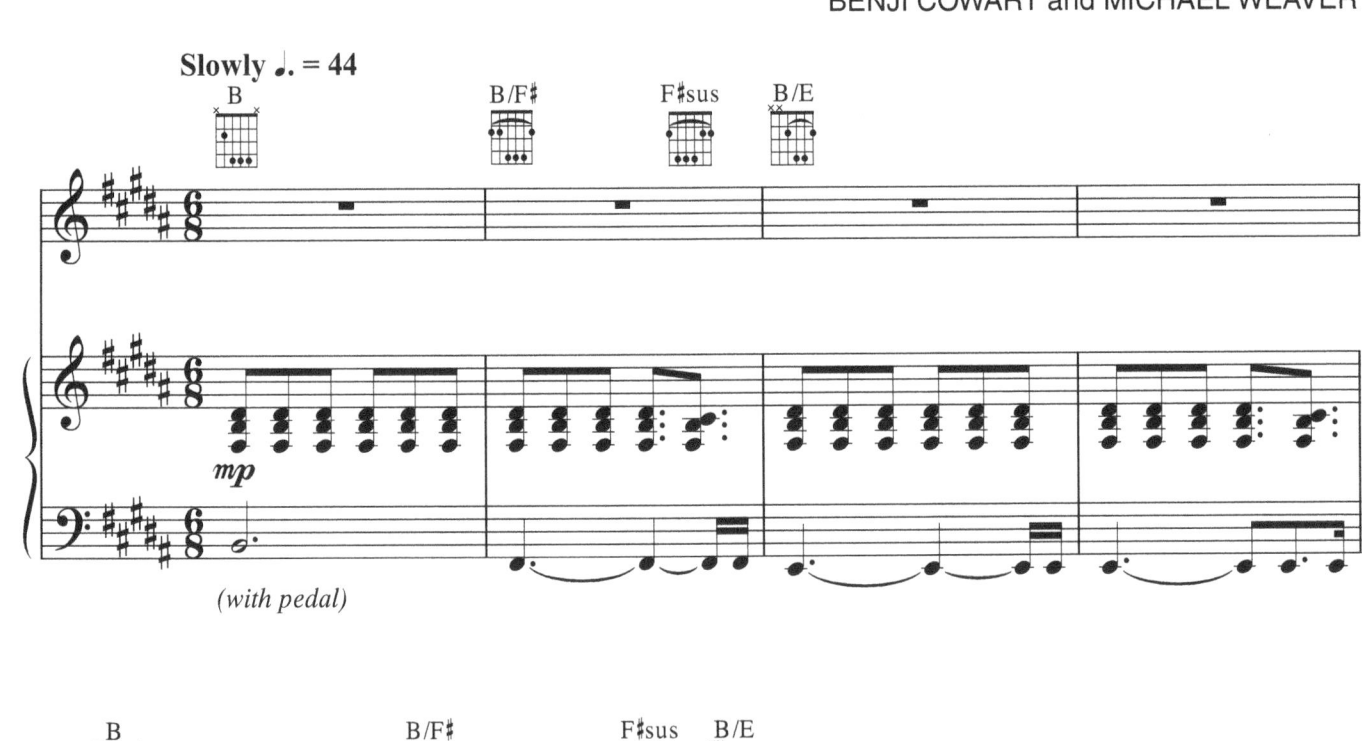

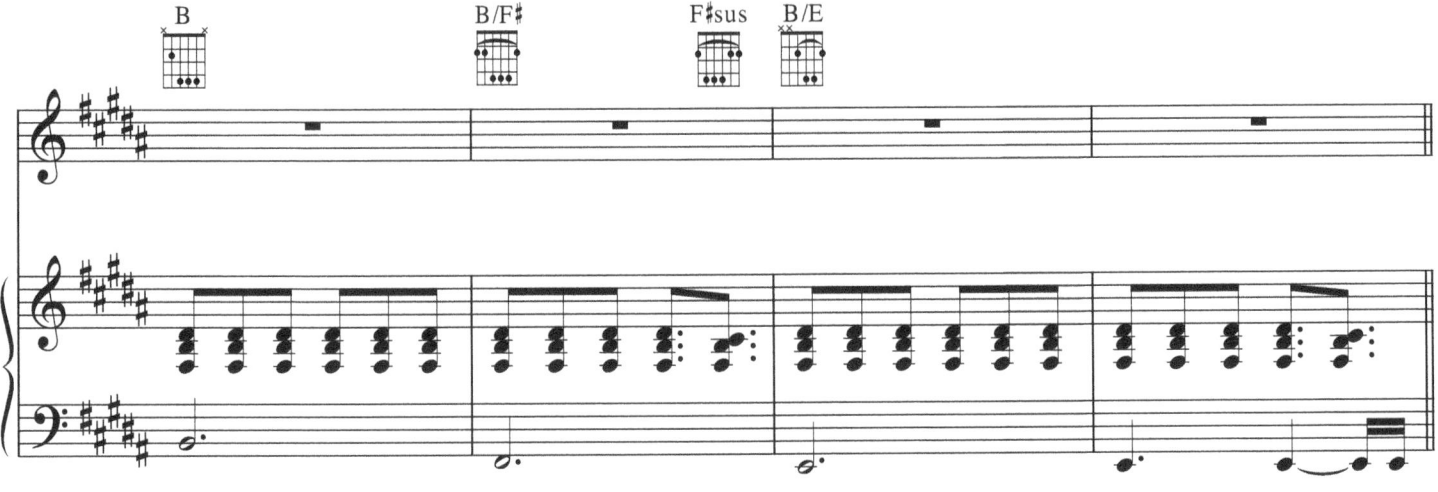

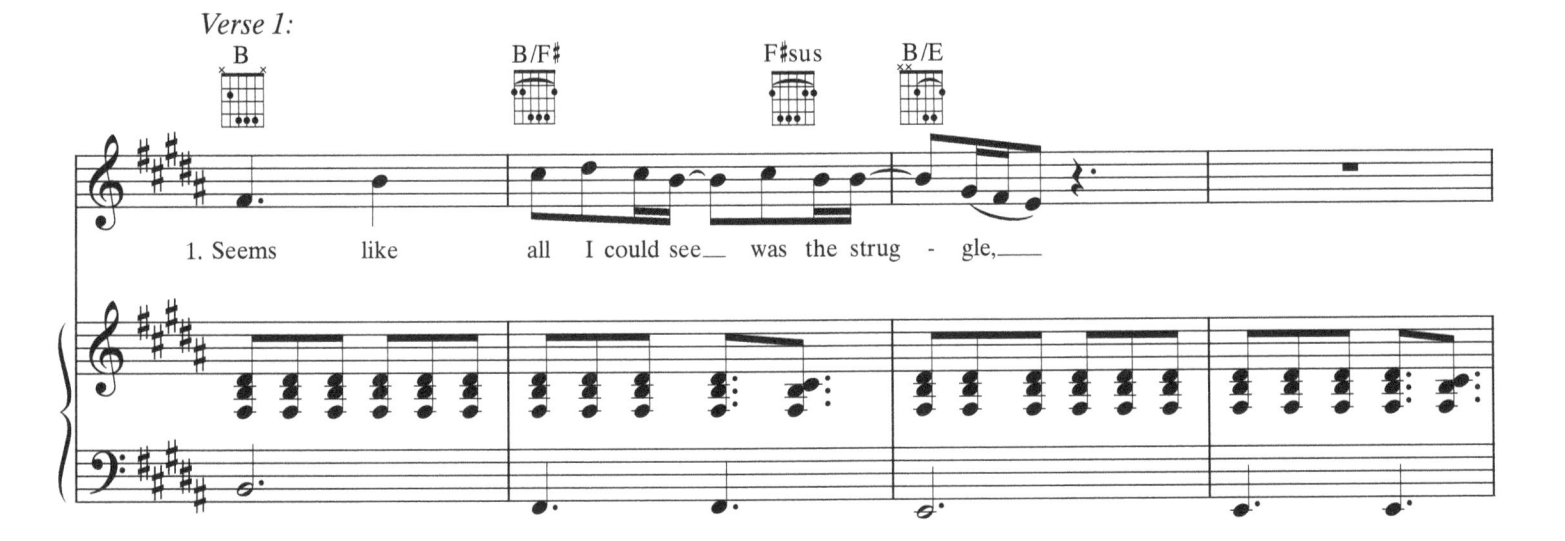

1. Seems like all I could see___ was the strug - gle,___

Verse 2:

2. All my life I have been called un - wor - thy, named by the voice of my shame and re - gret. But when I hear You whis - per, "Child, lift up your head," I re - mem - ber, O God, You're not done with me yet. I am re -

REVELATION SONG

Words and Music by
JENNIE LEE RIDDLE

Verse 2: (Sing first time only)

Verse 3: (Sing second time only)

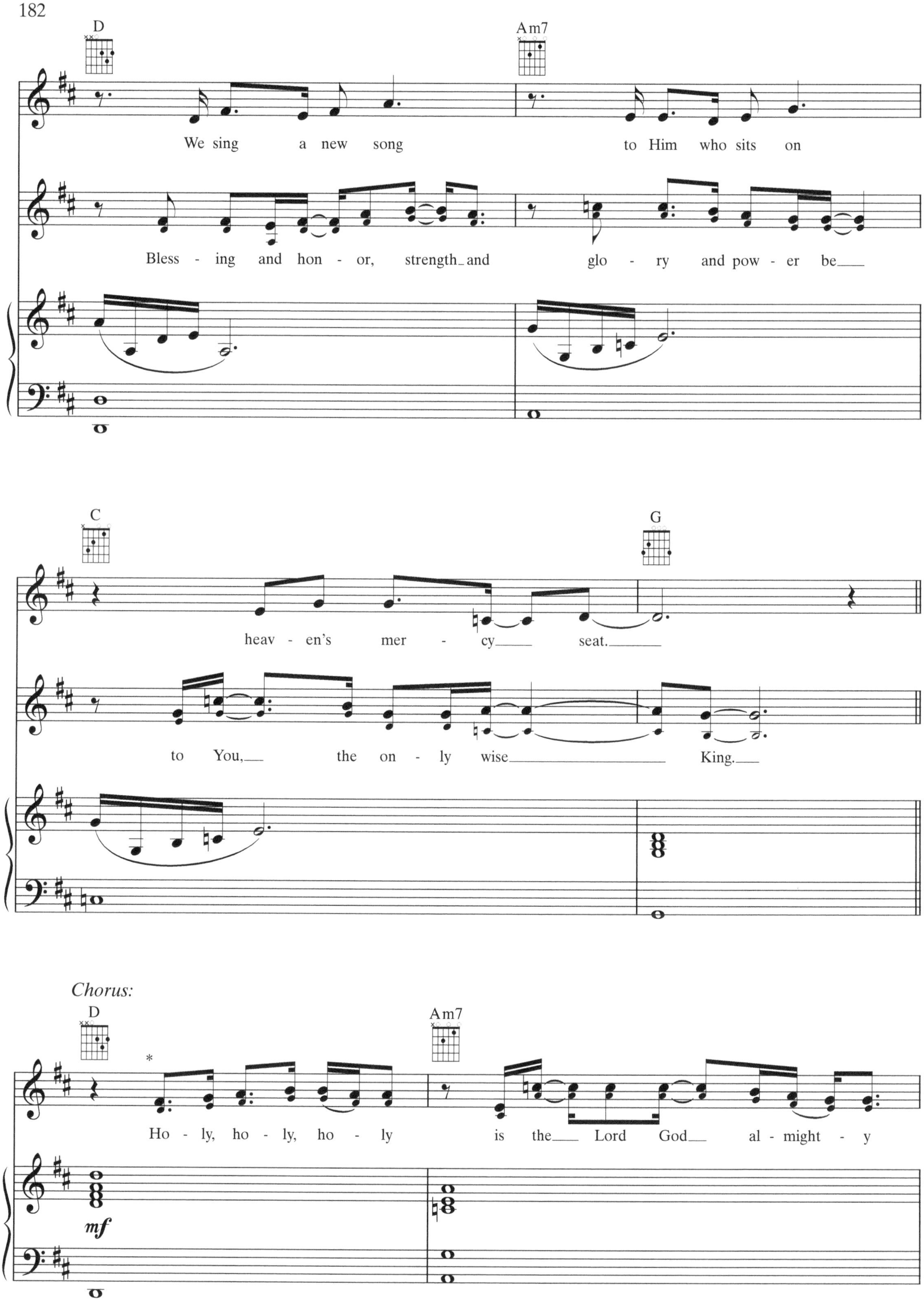
D
Am7
We sing a new song to Him who sits on
Bless - ing and hon - or, strength_and glo - ry and pow - er be
C
G
heav - en's mer - cy seat.
to You, the on - ly wise King.
Chorus:
D
Am7
*
Ho - ly, ho - ly, ho - ly is the Lord God al - might - y
mf

* *Harmony 2nd time only*

C

who was____ and is____ and is____ to come.____

G

D

With all cre-a-tion I____ sing,   "Praise to the King of kings;

Am7

C

You are my ev-'ry-thing   and I will____ a-dore You."____

G

1.
D

Am7

C(9)

G

SHOUT TO THE LORD

Words and Music by
DARLENE ZSCHECH

TAKE ME BACK

Words and Music by
ANDRAÉ CROUCH

Take Me Back - 5 - 1

take me back, dear Lord, where I first be-lieved.

lieved. I feel that I'm so far from You, Lord,

Verse:

Solo: (sung freely)

but still, I hear you call-ing me. Those sim-ple things

that I once knew, the mem-o-ries are draw-ing me.

TAKE ME TO THE KING

Words and Music by
KIRK FRANKLIN

200

Cb9   Db(9)

Lay me at the throne.___ Leave me there a - lone___

Db7   Gbmaj7

to gaze up - on___ Your glo - ry and sing to You___ this song.___

Cb9   Db

Please, take me to the King.___ 3. Truth is, it's___

Verse 3:

Bbm   Db

time_____ to stop playin' these_ games. We_ need a word.

mp

204

Take Me to the King - 8 - 7

WHO YOU ARE

Words and Music by
JASON WALKER, MICHAEL GOMEZ,
CHAD MATTSON and JON LOWRY

Chorus:

too__ hard, so__ fast, so__ far__ that you can't__ get back, when you're lost__ where you are. It's nev-er

too__ late, so__ bad, so__ much that you can't__ change who you are.

Ooo,_____ you can change who you are.

Ooo._____ You be-lieve_in free-__ So let the

WE ARE

Words and Music by
ED CASH, CHUCK BUTLER,
JAMES TEALY and HILLARY McBRIDE

We Are - 7 - 1

WHOM SHALL I FEAR
(GOD OF ANGEL ARMIES)

Words and Music by
CHRIS TOMLIN, ED CASH
and SCOTT CASH

*On the original recording, acoustic guitars play with capo 5.

Whom Shall I Fear (God of Angel Armies) - 7 - 1

YOU ARE

Words and Music by
RHYAN SHIRLEY, JARED MARTIN,
COLTON DIXON and MIKE BUSBEE

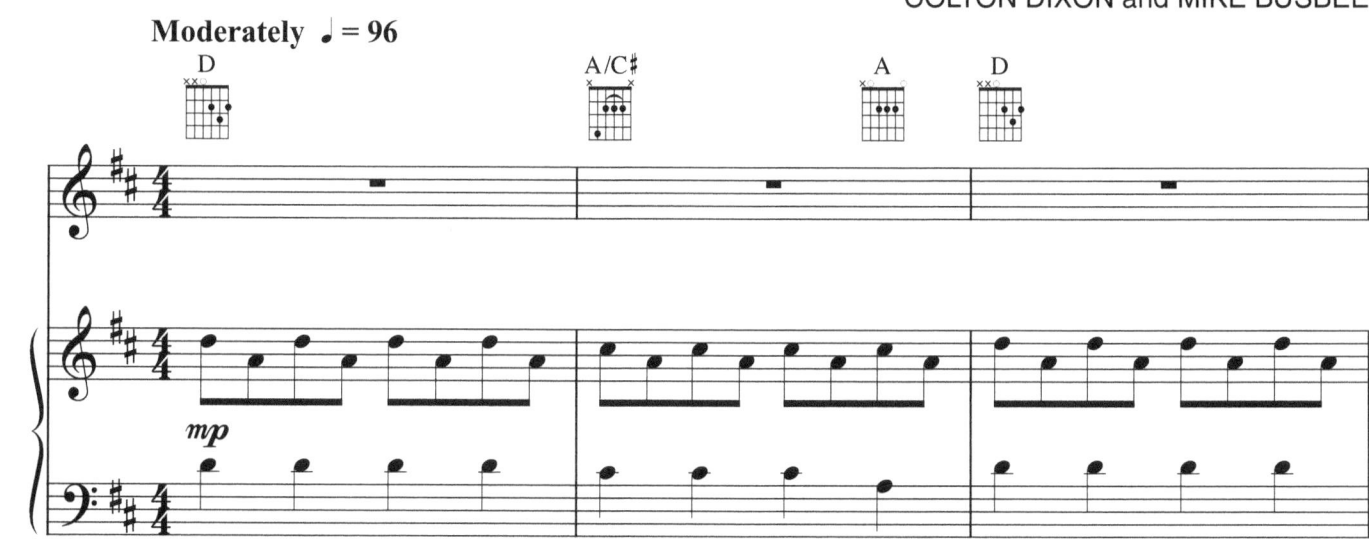

Verse 1:

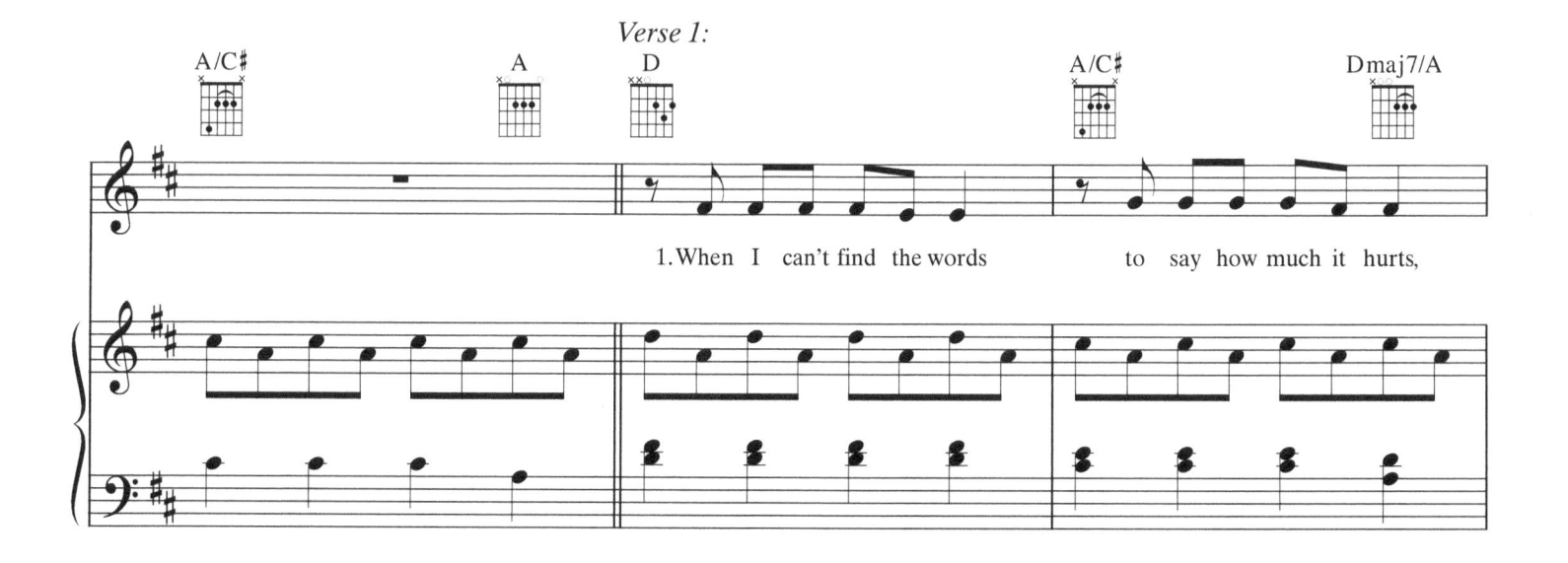

1.When I can't find the words to say how much it hurts,

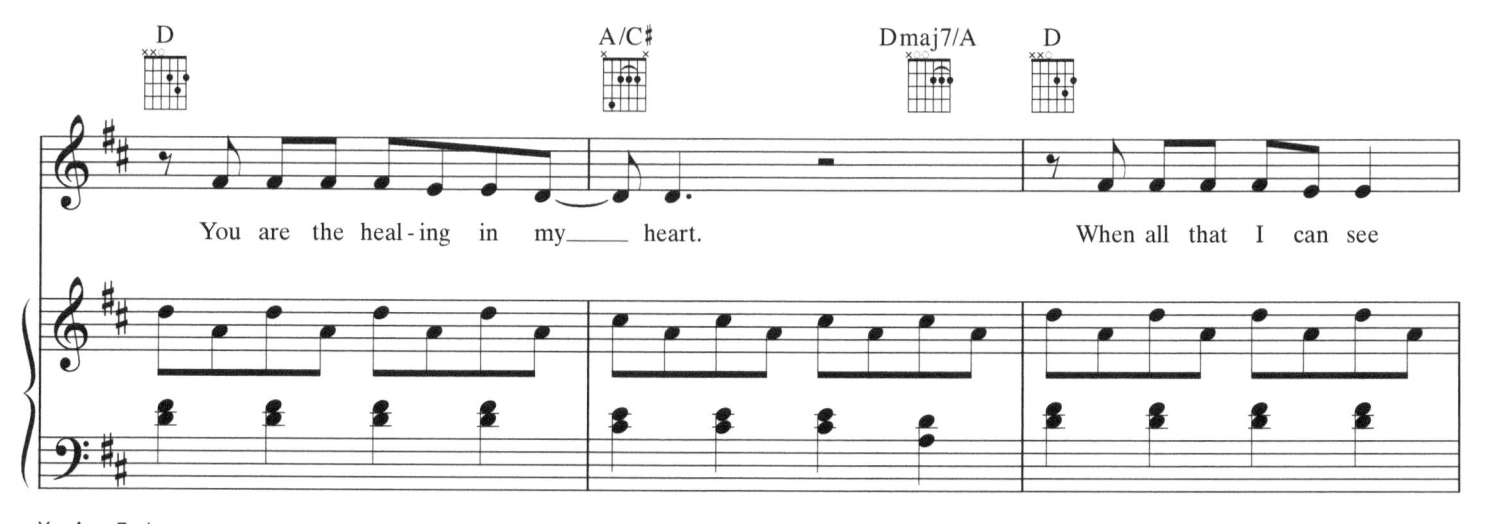

You are the heal-ing in my___ heart. When all that I can see

YOU RAISE ME UP

Words and Music by
ROLF LOVLAND and BRENDAN GRAHAM

You Raise Me Up - 5 - 1

YOUR LOVE NEVER FAILS

Words and Music by
ANTHONY SKINNER and CHRIS McCLARNEY

Moderate rock ♩ = 112

Oh oh oh___ oh oh___ oh___ oh___ oh.___

Verse 1:

1. Noth - ing___ can sep - a - rate, ev - en if I run a - way, Your___ love nev - er fails.___